EASY KEYBOARD HARMONY
Book FOUR
by WESLEY SCHAUM

FOREWORD

This series provides practical keyboard training leading into improvising an accompaniment from standard chord symbols — those commonly found in pop, folk, country, and sacred music — the same as used for guitar, organ, and piano accordion. Basic melody improvising is presented beginning in book 4.

A background of at least grade 1½ pianistic ability is necessary before starting book 1. Harmonic analysis is purposely avoided. It is intended that practical keyboard experience be allowed to develop prior to analytical work.

This fourth book presents the use of passing tones and neighboring tones in accompaniments. Melody improvising with chord tones, passing tones, and neighboring tones is introduced. Major 7th and minor 7th chords are taught in all keys.

RECOMMENDED SUPPLEMENTS

At least one album and several pieces of sheet music, with chord symbols, should be used to reinforce the chords, accompaniments, and improvising ideas taught here. The Schaum catalog includes many choices. Current popular tunes as well as hundreds of older pops (oldies but goodies) may also be used. The Schaum *Chord Speller* is recommended as a *workbook*.

When playing any music with chord symbols, read only the treble clef melody; bass clef notes are not used. The ▪ left hand is to improvise an accompaniment based on the chord symbols as taught in this series.

Ear training is to be encouraged. A very desirable side-effect of study in this book is to implant the *sound* of major, minor, augmented, 6th, 7th, etc. into memory.

CONTENTS

EXCLUSIVELY DISTRIBUTED BY

HAL•LEONARD®
CORPORATION
7777 W. BLUEMOUND RD. P.O. BOX 13819 MILWAUKEE, WI 53213

ISBN-13: 978-1-936098-20-0

01-44

LESSON 1: Passing Tones in 4/4 Accompaniments (Root Position)

Accompaniment patterns may include notes that are not chord tones. The *passing tone* is one type of non-chordal note which passes between chord tones connecting them in scale-like fashion. Arrows indicate the passing tones in the line below; notice that they may pass *upward* or *downward*. Similar passing tones can be added to root position triads in any key.

Keyboard Exercise: Practice the line below at least five times per day until it can be played easily and accurately.

Directions: Experiment by playing every measure of "Nelly Bly" with each of the passing tone patterns shown above. Write an accompaniment that sounds best with the melody; several measures have been filled in as samples. If none of the passing tone patterns seem to fit, write an ordinary broken chord accompaniment. Add an ending pattern in the final measure, then learn to play the entire piece.

NELLY BLY

LESSON 2: Passing Tones in 4/4 Accompaniments (Inversions)

The two lines below show possible accompaniment patterns for inversions of triads and 7th chords. Passing tones are indicated with arrows. Circled numbers correspond with measure numbers in "Yankee Doodle Dandy".

Keyboard Exercise: Practice the two lines below at least five times per day until they can be played easily and accurately.

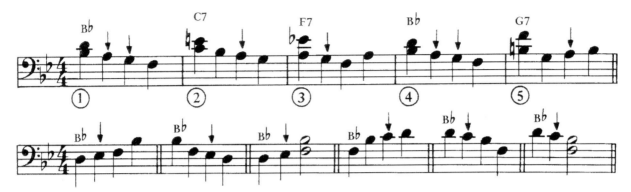

Directions: Write an accompaniment for "Yankee Doodle Dandy" using the samples in the first line above. Experiment by trying various passing tone accompaniments (either root position or inversions) for the remaining measures. Write an ending pattern in the final measure, then learn to play the entire piece.

YANKEE DOODLE DANDY

LESSON 3: Passing Tones in 3/4 Accompaniments

The first line below shows various passing tone patterns in 3/4 time for a root position triad. The 2nd line shows additional patterns for inversions of a triad. These can, of course, be adapted to any triad (major, minor, or augmented) in any key. Passing tones are indicated with arrows.

Keyboard Exercise: Practice the two lines below at least five times per day until they can be played easily and accurately.

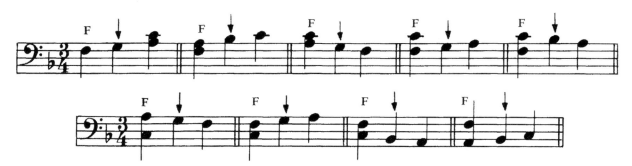

Directions: Write the accompaniment for "Beautiful Dreamer" using various passing tone patterns as shown in the lines above, then learn to play the entire piece. Several measures have been filled in as samples. A new ending pattern is shown in the last two measures. Similar endings can be invented using other passing tones. Passing tones are indicated with arrows.

BEAUTIFUL DREAMER

LESSON 4: Improvised Passing Tone Accompaniments

Passing tones may be added to nearly any broken chord pattern to form an improvised accompaniment. A study of the movement in the melody often suggests passing tones that can be used. Passing tones may move in *parallel motion* (same direction) or in *contrary motion* (opposite direction) with the melody. Several accompaniment patterns appear in the line below; passing tones are indicated with arrows.

Keyboard Exercise: Practice the line below at least five times per day until it can be played easily and accurately.

Directions: Experiment by playing various accompaniments shown above in each measure of "Song of Joy". You may create different passing tone patterns of your own. Write the accompaniment that seems to sound best with the melody. Add an ending pattern in the final measure, then learn to play the entire piece.

SONG OF JOY

LESSON 5: Chord Tones Added to Melody

Numerous accompaniments are possible when adding a chord tone below the melody (notes with stems down in treble clef). When playing two notes in the treble clef, the bass clef may have single note patterns with passing tones as indicated with arrows.

Directions: Experiment by adding chord tones below the melody and playing various passing tone patterns in each measure of "Faith of Our Fathers" (similar to the samples). You may, of course, create new patterns of your own. Write the accompaniment that seems to sound best with the melody. Add an ending pattern in the final measure, then learn to play the entire piece.

FAITH OF OUR FATHERS

Lesson 5 — continued

Treble clef notes, with stems down, indicate chord tones which have been added below the melody of "Gypsy Love Song". Passing tones are indicated with arrows in the sample measures of the bass clef. Although there are many opportunities for passing tone accompaniments, you may prefer to use ordinary broken chord patterns for some measures.

Directions: Experiment by adding chord tones below the melody and playing various passing tone accompaniment patterns in each measure of "Gypsy Love Song" (similar to the samples). You may create other patterns of your own. Write the accompaniment that seems to sound best with the melody. Add an ending pattern in the final two measures, then learn to play the entire piece.

GYPSY LOVE SONG

LESSON 6: Passing Tones Between Accompaniment Chords

Passing tones may be used to connect any accompaniment chords as illustrated by arrows in the two lines below. Notice that the passing note must not be *any* chord tone of *either* chord immediately before or after. The circled numbers correspond to measures in "Sometimes I Feel Like a Motherless Child".

Keyboard Exercise: Practice the two lines below at least five times per day until they can be played easily and accurately.

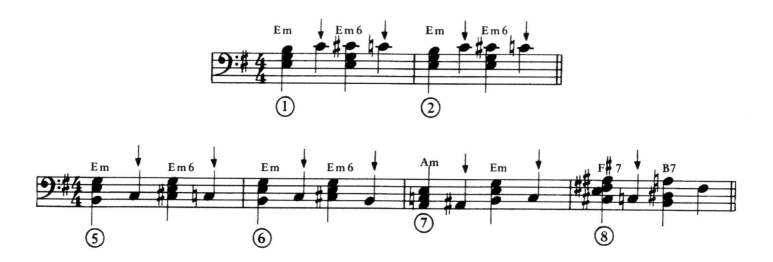

Directions: Write the accompaniment for "Sometimes I Feel Like a Motherless Child" using the samples from the two lines above. For the remaining measures, play the chords indicated on the 1st and 3rd beats, one at a time with the melody. Experiment to see if any passing tones could be used to lead from one chord to the next. If no passing tones fit with root position, try each inversion. The passing tones should sound good with the melody, although a mild dissonance may be desirable for added color and flavor. Add an ending pattern in the final measure, then learn to play the entire piece.

SOMETIMES I FEEL LIKE A MOTHERLESS CHILD

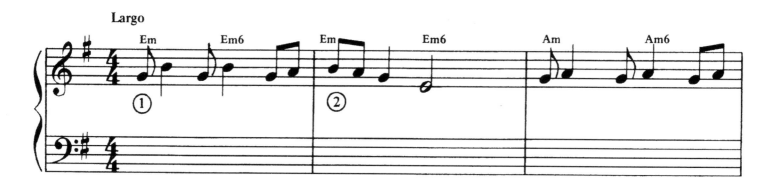

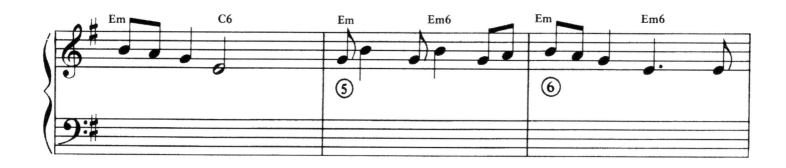

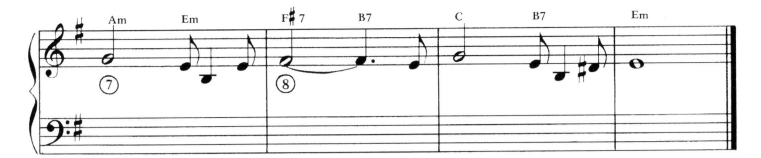

Passing tones are indicated with arrows in the line below. The circled number indicates the measure number in "Merrily We Roll Along".

Keyboard Exercise: Practice the line below at least five times per day until it can be played easily and accurately.

Directions: Write the accompaniment for "Merrily We Roll Along" using the sample from the line above. Experiment with passing tones in the remaining measures (explained on page 8). Add an ending pattern in the final measure, then learn to play the entire piece.

MERRILY WE ROLL ALONG

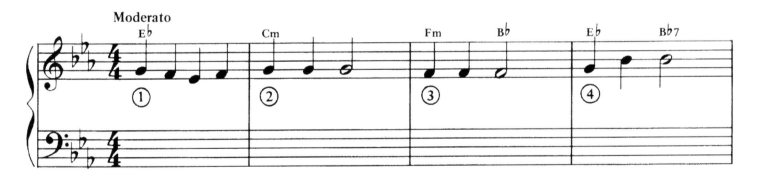

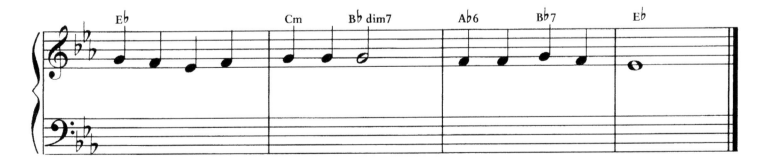

Special Note: The chords, accompaniments and improvising ideas taught in this book should also be used in at least one supplementary album and several pieces of sheet music, with chord symbols. The Schaum catalog includes many choices. Current popular tunes as well as hundreds of older pops (oldies but goodies) may also be used. The Schaum *Chord Speller* is recommended as a *workbook*.

When playing any music with chord symbols, read only the treble clef melody; bass clef notes are not used. The left hand is to improvise an accompaniment based on the chord symbols as taught in this series.

Lesson 6 — continued

Passing tones are indicated with arrows in the two lines below. The circled numbers indicate measure numbers in "Come, Thou Almighty King". Notice that the passing notes in measures 12 and 14 are somewhat different because of the broken chord pattern on the 1st and 2nd counts.

Keyboard Exercise: Practice the two lines below at least five times per day until they can be played easily and accurately.

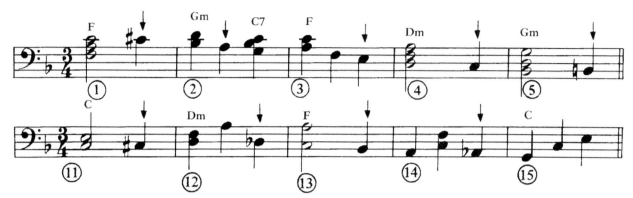

Directions: Write the accompaniment for "Come, Thou Almighty King" using the samples from the lines above. Experiment with passing tones in the remaining measures. Add an ending pattern in the final measure, then learn to play the entire piece.

COME, THOU ALMIGHTY KING

Lesson 6 — continued

Passing tones are indicated with arrows in the two lines below. The circled numbers indicate measure numbers in "By the Moon's Pale Light". Notice the *double* passing notes in measures 5, 6, and 9.

Keyboard Exercise: Practice the two lines below at least five times per day until they can be played easily and accurately.

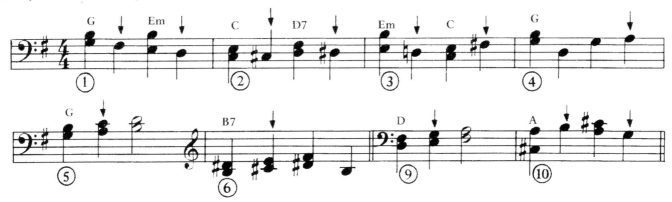

Directions: Write the accompaniment for "By the Moon's Pale Light" using the samples from the lines above. Experiment with passing tones in the remaining measures. Add an ending pattern in the final measure, then learn to play the entire piece.

BY THE MOON'S PALE LIGHT

LESSON 7: Neighboring Tones Within Chords

The *neighboring tone* is another important non-chordal tone often used in accompaniment patterns. It is *preceded* and *followed* by the same chord tone and may move above or below that chord tone. Arrows indicate various neighboring tones in the line below. Circled numbers correspond to measures in "John Jacob Jingleheimer Schmidt". Notice how chord tones have been added below the melody notes.

Keyboard Exercise: Practice the line below at least five times per day until it can be played easily and accurately.

Directions: Write the accompaniment for "John Jacob Jingleheimer Schmidt" using the samples shown in the line above. Experiment with added chord tones below melody notes and with different neighboring tone patterns in all remaining measures. Try neighboring tones on all notes of each chord to see which sounds best with the melody. If no neighboring tones seem to fit, write an ordinary broken chord accompaniment. Improvise an ending by changing the melody and chords in the last two measures (see Section X on back reference page), then learn to play the entire piece.

JOHN JACOB JINGLEHEIMER SCHMIDT

Lesson 7 — continued

The two lines below illustrate various 3/4 accompaniment patterns; neighboring tones are indicated with arrows. Circled numbers correspond with measures in "Sweet Rosie O'Grady".

Keyboard Exercise: Practice the two lines below at least five times per day until they can be played easily and accurately.

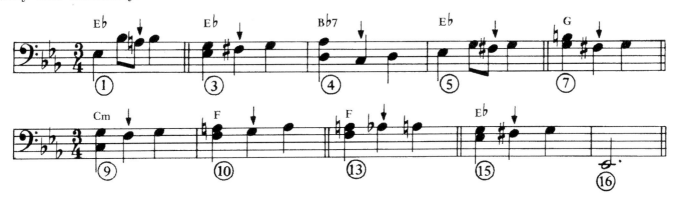

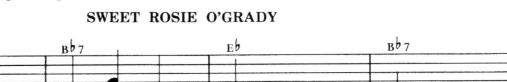

Directions: Write the accompaniment for "Sweet Rosie O'Grady" using the samples you like from the two lines above. Experiment with different neighboring tone patterns in all remaining measures. If none of the neighboring tones seem to fit, experiment with passing tones or use a broken chord accompaniment, then learn to play the entire piece. The bass clef notes printed in the last two measures above show a simple neighboring tone *ending pattern.*

SWEET ROSIE O'GRADY

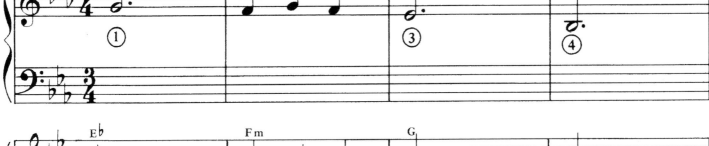

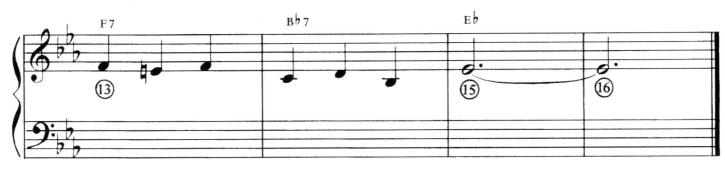

LESSON 8: Additional Neighboring Tone Accompaniments

Neighboring tones may be used with any chord tone of any accompaniment chord as illustrated by arrows in the lines below. The 2nd line shows variations where the neighboring tones are preceded by a *skip* rather than an adjacent chord tone. Many additional accompaniment patterns can be devised using rhythmic variations. Different neighboring tone patterns help add variety to the accompaniment when the same chord is used for several measures in a row as in "Bill Bailey".

Keyboard Exercise: Practice the two lines below at least five times per day until they can be played easily and accurately.

Directions: Experiment by playing various neighboring tone patterns with "Bill Bailey". You may invent other accompaniments of your own. In some cases, you may prefer to use ordinary broken chord patterns. Write those that sound best with the melody. In measures 7-8 and 15-16, the accompaniment has been printed to show "fill-in" possibilities using neighboring tones. Experiment with different neighboring tones to form an ending in the last two measures, then learn to play the entire piece.

BILL BAILEY, WON'T YOU PLEASE COME HOME

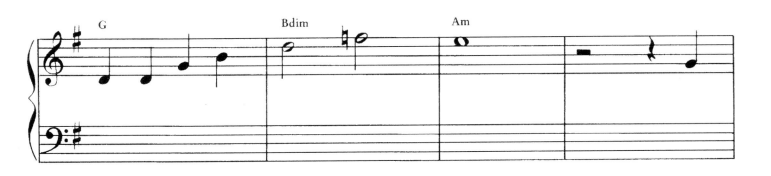

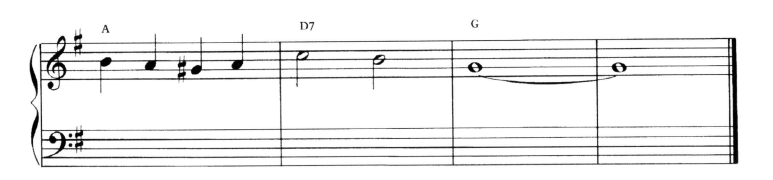

LESSON 9: Major 7th Chords (Sharp Keys)

Chords are formed from the notes of the major scale. C chords are based on the C major scale; G chords are based on the G major scale, etc. The numbers used in chord symbols refer to specific notes of the major scale called *degrees*. For example, the 3rd *degree* is the 3rd *note* of the major scale.

A major 7th chord is formed by adding the 7th degree of the major scale to any major triad. The chord symbol is CM7 (with *capital* "M"), CMaj7, or Cmaj7.

The line below shows the first 7 notes *(degrees)* of the C major scale, a C major triad, and CM7 chord with two accompaniment patterns. The last measure compares the CM7 and C7*.

Keyboard Exercise: Practice the line below at least five times per day until it can be played easily and accurately.

Directions: Write a major 7th chord or regular 7th chord beneath the appropriate chord symbols below, using the line above as a sample. Then write two different accompaniment patterns for each major 7th chord. Refer to the chord dictionary (front reference page) if necessary.

Keyboard Exercise: After completing the written work, practice each line above at least five times per day until it can be played easily and accurately. Additional accompaniment patterns may also be practiced, if desired.

* The "regular" 7th chord uses a *lowered* 7th degree of the major scale.

Lesson 9 — continued

Various accompaniment patterns for major 7th chords in both 4/4 and 3/4 time may be adapted from the regular 7th chord accompaniments shown in section IX on the back reference page.

Major 7th chords are often used as substitutes for major triads or major 6th chords. In "The Year of Jubilo", major 7th chords have been used to add extra color and flavor to the harmony.

Directions: Write the accompaniment for "The Year of Jubilo", using the first two measures as a sample. Experiment by trying root position and various inversions of each chord. Choose the ones that sound best with the melody and which minimize jumping from one chord to another.

THE YEAR OF JUBILO

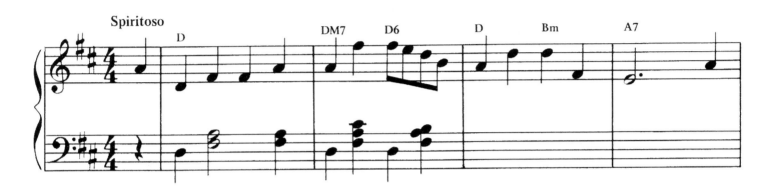

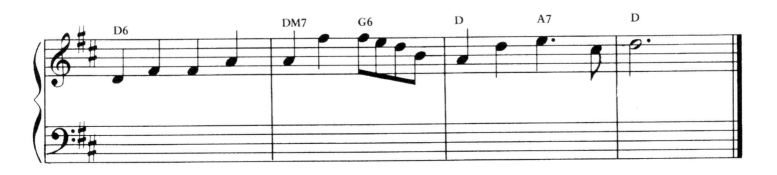

LESSON 10: Major 7th Chords (Flat Keys)

Shown in the line below are the first 7 notes of the F major scale, an F major triad, and FM7 chord with two accompaniment patterns. The last measure compares the FM7 and F7.

Keyboard Exercise: Practice the line below at least five times per day until it can be played easily and accurately.

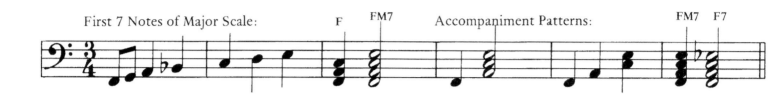

Directions: Write a major 7th chord or regular 7th chord beneath the appropriate chord symbols below, using the line above as a sample. Then write two different accompaniment patterns for each major 7th chord. Refer to the chord dictionary (front reference page) if necessary.

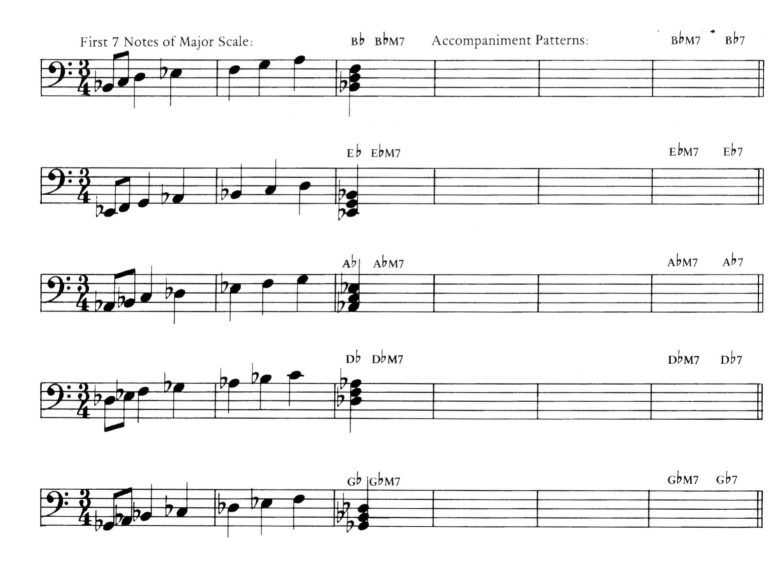

Keyboard Exercise: After completing the written work, practice each line above at least five times per day until it can be played easily and accurately.

Special Note: Additional accompaniment patterns for major 7th chords, both 3/4 and 4/4, can be adapted from the 7th chord patterns shown in section IX on the back reference page.

Lesson 10 — continued

A major 7th chord in sequence with a major 6th chord makes a nice variation to use in place of a plain major triad in several successive measures. The line below has sequences — major triad, major 7th, major 6th — for the A-flat and E-flat chords. Either sequence could also be used as an *ending pattern*.

Keyboard Exercise: Practice the line below at least five times per day until it can be played easily and accurately.

Directions: Write the accompaniment for "On Top of Old Smoky". Use a sequence like those shown in the line above, in measures 2-3-4, 6-7-8, and 14-15-16. Write the chord symbols you use above measures 3-4, 7-8, and 15-16; then learn to play the entire piece.

ON TOP OF OLD SMOKY

LESSON 11: Minor 7th Chords (Sharp Keys)

Common 7th chords (C7, G7, F#7, etc.) are sometimes called *dominant* 7ths to distinguish them from various other forms of 7ths. Any dominant 7th chord may be changed into a *minor* 7th by lowering the 3rd degree one chromatic half-step, as you would to form a minor triad. The chord symbol is Cm7 (with *small* "m").

The line below shows a C7 chord followed by a Cm7 and two accompaniment patterns. After the double bar, a Cm7 is shown in root position and its three inversions.

Keyboard Exercise: Practice the line below at least five times per day until it can be played easily and accurately. This line may be played one octave higher if desired.

Directions: Write a minor 7th chord followed by two accompaniment patterns in the blank spaces below, using the line above as a sample. After the double bar, write accidentals as necessary to form the root position and three inversions of the minor 7th chord. Refer to the chord dictionary (front reference page) if necessary.

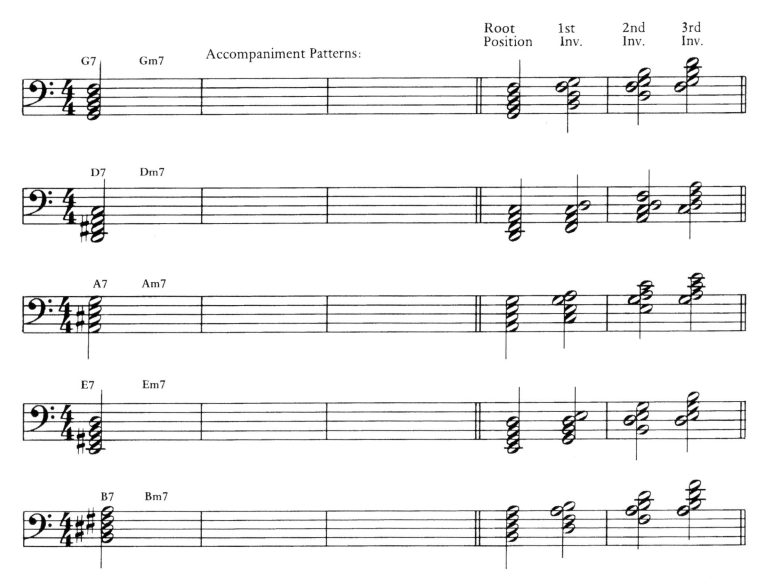

Keyboard Exercise: After completing the written work, practice each line above at least five times per day until it can be played easily and accurately. Any line may be played one octave higher, if desired.

Special Note: Additional accompaniment patterns for minor 7th chords, both 4/4 and 3/4, can be adapted from the 7th chord patterns shown in section IX on the back reference page.

Lesson 11 — continued

Pieces originally harmonized with plain chords and rather few chord changes can often be given new vitality by substituting and making added chord changes as shown in this version of "Home, Sweet Home". Minor 7th chords may often be substituted for minor triads; major 7ths may be substituted for major triads.

A more professional sound is achieved by using a mixture of root position and inversions to avoid wide jumps from one chord to another. This is illustrated in the line below where circled chord symbols indicate inversions.

Keyboard Exercise: Practice the line below at least five times per day until it can be played easily and accurately.

Directions: Write an accompaniment for "Home, Sweet Home"; the sample line above may be used for the 2nd line of "Home, Sweet Home". Use an ending pattern in the final measure; then learn to play the entire piece.

HOME, SWEET HOME

LESSON 12: Minor 7th Chords (Flat Keys)

The line below shows an F7 chord followed by an Fm7 and two accompaniment patterns. After the double bar, an Fm7 is shown in root position and its three inversions.

Keyboard Exercise: Practice the line below at least five times per day until it can be played easily and accurately. This line may be played one octave higher if desired.

Directions: Write a minor 7th chord followed by two accompaniment patterns in the blank spaces below, using the line above as a sample. After the double bar, write accidentals where necessary to form the root position and three inversions of the minor 7th chord. Refer to the chord dictionary (front reference page) if necessary.

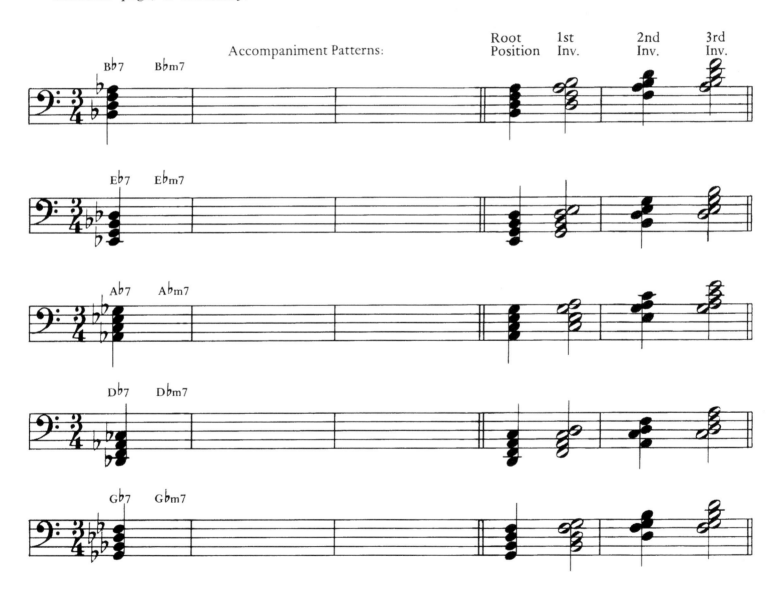

Keyboard Exercise: After completing the written work, practice each line above at least five times per day until it can be played easily and accurately. Any line may be played one octave higher if desired.

Special Note: Inversions of minor 7th chords *sound* the same and are *spelled* the same as major 6th chords and their inversions. For example, an Fm7 chord sounds the same as an A-flat 6th chord; the only difference is the *root*. For this reason, minor 7th and major 6th chords sound best when used in *root position*. Although any inversion may be used, give preference to root positions of these chords when possible.

Lesson 12 — continued

The melody for the first 8 measures of "The Ash Grove" is the same as the last 8 measures. Notice the use of *different* chords during the repetition to give added variety. This same idea can often be used in other pieces of music with portions of melody that are repeated or nearly the same.

Directions: Write the accompaniment for "The Ash Grove" using root position and inversions to achieve a smooth flow in the left hand. Add an ending pattern in the last measure, then learn to play the entire piece.

THE ASH GROVE

LESSON 13: Melody Improvising with Chord Tones (3/4)

Chord tones may be added as improvised notes to fill-in when the melody is a half note or longer. Plain or fancy fill-ins can be formed by using different rhythms. The three lines below show several possible fill-ins for the same melodic segments. Melody notes are full size, improvised notes are small. Circled numbers refer to measures in "Spring, Sweet Spring".

Keyboard Exercise: Practice the three lines below at least five times per day until they can be played easily and accurately.

Directions: Experiment by playing various accompaniments with all of the different fill-ins shown above. Many of the same fill-ins can be used in later measures of "Spring, Sweet Spring". It is not necessary to use melody fill-ins with every measure. A variety of melody fill-ins, accompaniment fill-ins, and ordinary broken chord accompaniments creates a more interesting style. Write the fill-ins you like best along with a suitable accompaniment. You may also improvise other fill-ins of your own, then learn to play the entire piece.

SPRING, SWEET SPRING

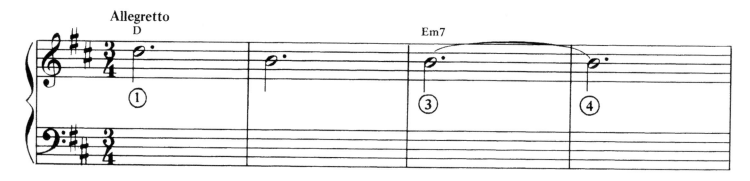

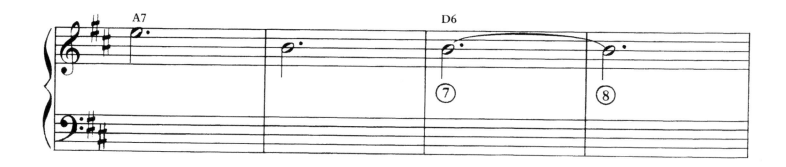

LESSON 14: Melody Improvising with Chord Tones (4/4)

A variety of fill-ins based on chord tones is shown in the three lines below. Each line illustrates three different fill-ins for the same melodic segment. Melody notes are full size, improvised notes are small. Circled numbers refer to measures in "Andantino".

Keyboard Exercise: Practice the three lines below at least five times per day until they can be played easily and accurately.

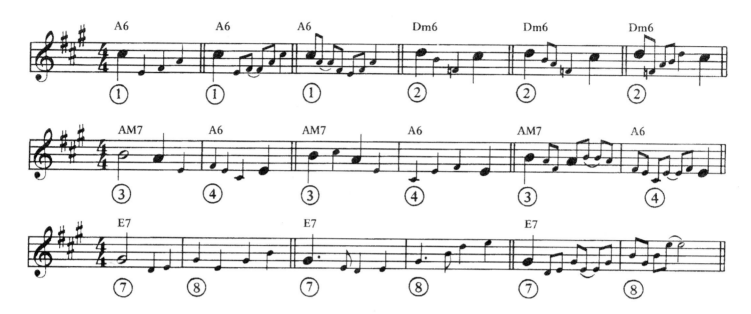

In many pieces, syncopated "pop style" 8th notes sound better than the strict "classic style". You may choose the style that seems better.

Directions: Experiment by playing various accompaniments with all of the different fill-ins shown above. Many of the same fill-ins can be used in later measures of "Andantino". Write the fill-ins you like best along with suitable accompaniments throughout. You may improvise different fill-ins of your own, then learn to play the entire piece.

ANDANTINO

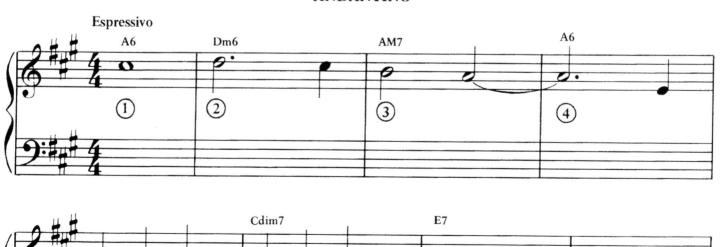

LESSON 15: Melody Improvising with Passing and Neighboring Tones (3/4)

A frequently used method of improvising is to add chord tones, passing tones, and neighboring tones *between* melody notes. This serves to "fill-in" places where there is no activity in the melody such as sustained notes, ties, or rests. Obviously, the fill-in notes must fit in with the melody in adjoining measures and sound well with the chord accompaniment.

The three lines below show many possible fill-in patterns for the dotted half notes in "Heart of My Heart". The first line has simple quarter note rhythms, the 2nd and 3rd lines have various 8th note rhythms. Melody notes are printed full size, *improvised* notes are *small*. Circled numbers refer to measures in "Heart of My Heart". Neighboring tones and passing tone are indicated by arrows. Other small notes are chord tones from the chord symbol in each measure.

Keyboard Exercise: Practice the three lines below at least five times per day until they can be played easily and accurately.

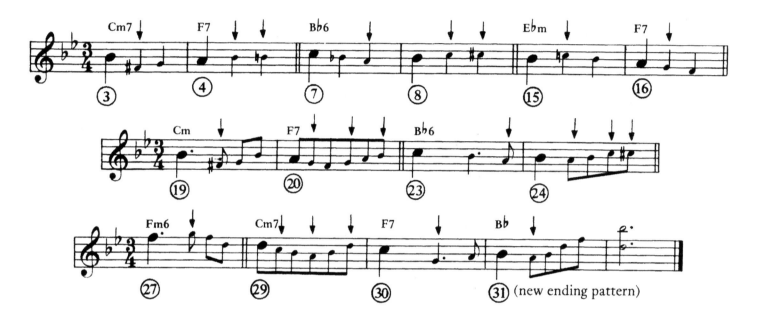

Directions: Experiment with fill-in notes in all measures of "Heart of My Heart" that contain dotted half notes, selecting from the samples above and improvising other patterns of your own. Write those fill-ins that fit with the melody in adjoining measures. Experiment with various accompaniments; write those that sound good with the melody and fill-in notes, then learn to play the entire piece.

HEART OF MY HEART

LESSON 16: Melody Improvising with Passing and Neighboring Tones (4/4)

Improvised notes may often be added to the melody where half notes or longer note values appear. Various rhythms and syncopations offer many possibilities as shown in the three lines below. Melody notes are full size, improvised notes are *small*. Arrows indicate neighboring tones and passing tones. Other small notes are chord tones from the chord symbol in each measure. Circled numbers refer to measures in "Jingle Bells".

Keyboard Exercise: Practice the three lines below at least five times per day until they can be played easily and accurately.

Directions: Experiment with fill-in notes in all measures of "Jingle Bells" that contain half notes and longer note values. Select from the samples above and improvise other patterns of your own. Write those fill-ins that fit with the melody in adjoining measures. Experiment with various accompaniments; write those that sound good with the melody and fill-in notes, then learn to play the entire piece.

JINGLE BELLS

REFERENCE PAGE *(see front and back inside covers for additional information)*

II. CHORD SUBSTITUTE DIRECTORY

Until a wider range of chords is learned in later books of this series, substitute chords may be selected from the dictionary on the front inside cover. (C chords are listed as samples; similar substitutes may be made in *any key*.)

Please note: A *flat* is sometimes used in place of a *minus* sign.

For C7sus4, C7-9, C9, C11, C11-9, C11+, C13, or C13-9 .... substitute = C7

For C7-5 or C9-5 .... substitute = C7 or Cdim7 (C°7)

For C7+5, C+7, or C9+5 .... substitute = Caug (C+)

For Cm7-5 .... substitute = Cm7 or Cdim7 (C°7)

For C7/6 .... substitute = C7 or C6   For Cmaj9 (CM9) .... substitute = Cmaj7 (CM7)

For C9/6 .... substitute = C6   For Cm9 .... substitute = Cm7

III. 4/4 TRIAD ACCOMPANIMENT PATTERNS

The 4/4 patterns shown below may be used for all major, minor, diminished, and augmented triads in *any key*. The rhythms shown here can be adapted to *all inversions* of any triad, see Section IV, below. The arrows in the 3rd line point to alternate bass notes used with different rhythms. Additional accompaniment patterns are presented in later books of this series.

IV. 4/4 INVERSIONS of TRIADS

The basic broken chord patterns shown for the 1st and 2nd inversions may be adapted to any of the rhythms for root position, as shown in Section III.

V. 3/4 TRIAD ACCOMPANIMENT PATTERNS

The 3/4 patterns shown below may be used for all major, minor, diminished, and augmented triads in *any key*. Additional accompaniment patterns are presented in later books of this series.

VI. 3/4 INVERSIONS OF TRIADS

The basic broken chord patterns shown for the 1st and 2nd inversions below may be adapted to any of the rhythms for root position, as shown in Section V.